THE
MITTEN
BOOK

THE MITTEN BOOK

Inger Gottfridsson   Ingrid Gottfridsson

Lark Books
Asheville, North Carolina

Published in 1987, 1991 by Lark Books,
50 College Street
Asheville, North Carolina 28801

First published in Sweden under the title *Gotlandska Stickmonster*
© Inger Gottfridsson and Ingrid Gottfridsson
Almqvist & Wiksell Forlag AB, Stockholm 1981

Published in 1984 by Lark Books under the title *The Swedish Mitten Book*

English translation © 1984 by
Lark Books

ISBN 0-937274-36-4

Printed by South Sea International Press Ltd., Hong Kong

Contents

"How would it look, do you think, if everyone, old and young, would sit down together to knit for a while? Laughter and merriment and riddles and questions and folktales and anecdotes from each person's life would blend together in the stitches. Then later, when you recalled these events that have gone through your own fingers stitch by stitch, they would speak their own quiet language: Do you remember? Do you remember?"

—Hermanna Stengard

Knitting on Gotland

Hermanna Stengard has preserved for us a collection of old, wonderful knitting patterns that are tied to a tradition going far back in time. The patterns, unique to Gotland, were collected during her research all around the island, and were presented in her book *Gotlandsk Sticksom (The Knitting of Gotland)*, published in 1925.

Hermanna Stengard was born in 1861 and was an elementary school teacher on Gotland. Through her life-long interest in knitting and its history she also collected a treasury of folktales and stories relating to knitting, which inspire us to follow her entreaty to the people of Gotland: "To all old knitting artists who live here, to those who cherish the traditional art of Gotland as a valuable jewel, and to all who appreciate keeping this art, I make a warm appeal not to weary. Let us help each other to save the scraps so they are not wasted."

Her book, *Gotlandsk Sticksom*, is no longer in print. We feel it is important to make the old patterns available once again.

Trade with wool and knitted garments

The island of Gotland lies southeast of Sweden in the Baltic Sea. Today it is primarily a holiday resort for Stockholmers and a tourist attraction popular for its splendid old churches, but during the late Middle Ages Gotland was a major northern European trade center. Visby, its picturesque capitol, was one of the chief towns in the Hanseatic League. The craft of knitting came to Gotland earlier than to other parts of Scandinavia because of this foreign trade.

Most of the garments knitted for export were sweaters, but smaller garments, such as mittens and stockings, also were sold. Much of the exported knitwear was shipped across the sea to Stockholm, and many of the garments went to Russia and Germany too.

Both wool and knitted garments were used by the people on Gotland as a medium of exchange, beginning in the 17th century when tradesmen from the Swedish mainland came to sell their wares. These tradesmen resold the Gotland sweaters all across Sweden, and the beautiful designs became popular even in the northernmost parts of the country.

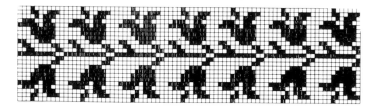

The "sweaterhags"

The "sweaterhags," as they called themselves, were women of all ages who gathered knitted goods from around the countryside and brought them to Visby to sell. Once a year, in the autumn, the sweaterhags traveled across the sea to Stockholm to sell Gotland's knitwear. One sweaterhag would bring along as many as 800 sweaters—perhaps 100 of which she had knitted herself. In addition, she would take stockings and smaller garments made by other knitters. A selection of other valuable goods was included in the cargo: mutton, wool, walnuts, and lavender. Once all trading in Stockholm was finished, the sweaterhags returned to Gotland in good time for the Christmas holidays.

The boat trip across the Baltic Sea was often hazardous because of autumn storms, and each year the sweaterhags left Gotland with their lives at stake. The trip in the fall of 1824 was especially memorable. As the boat began its return trip from Stockholm in early November, a severe storm broke out. The boat was tossed about in the terrible weather. It drifted off course and eventually came ashore at Osel, on the Estonian coast. After a month the weather improved enough to permit the return trip to Gotland and on Christmas Eve the boat sailed into the harbor. It was a joyous occasion for those waiting on shore, to once again greet friends and relatives who had been mourned as dead.

The preparation and dyeing of wool

Sheep have existed on Gotland for a very long time, and wool has naturally been the most important raw fiber.

Processing of the wool was traditionally done by women. The tasks were many and time-consuming, so women often did the chores together.

The first step was to card the wool coarsely and mix it for desired shades. The wool was then put into sacks and stored until it was time to fine-card it. It was then spun into yarn, and, finally, the yarn was dyed.

Most of the dyes were taken straight from nature. Juniper, oak bark, walnuts, chamomile, and different kinds of lichens were used. The lichens, harvested from old fences and rocks, are called "thinmoss" and "stonemoss" on Gotland.

Juniper and oak bark produced a gray color; chamomile and thinmoss, yellow. Thinmoss was mixed with iron vitriol to give an even, brown color. Stonemoss dyed the yarn a beautiful red-brown, named "stonemoss brown" for the plant.

Indigo and woad were used for blue. Indigo was imported from other countries. Woad was, at one time, a fairly common plant on Gotland. Carl von Linne, upon visiting a small island just east of Gotland, reported: "Woad, the very useful dye grass which, until now, has been considered rare in Sweden, was growing on the shore . . . . On the embankment was Woad growing all along the island as on a field of hemp."

To dye the yarn green, it was first dyed yellow with

angsskara, a daisy-like flower, then dipped in indigo. An aqua color was obtained by dipping the yellow yarn into a bath made of vinegar and salt which had been stored in a copper pot.

Cochineal, aniline, or madder was used for red. Madder was cultivated with great success on Gotland in the 18th century, but today it is scarce on the island.

Sheep were sheared in spring and fall. Yarn to be used for knitting was taken from the spring wool, then spun during the fall months to be ready for Christmas. The days between Christmas and Twelfth Night were special knitting holidays. During that time one was not permitted to use the spinning wheel or drop spindle because, according to popular belief, to do so meant the sheep would not thrive. Instead, holiday knitting guilds were held.

No woman was allowed to be idle and her knitting was always at hand, to be picked up at any spare moment. But it was also customary for men and children to help with knitting. There is a story about a Swedish army officer who was captured and taken to Siberia. Eventually he made his way to Gotland and arrived destitute. He settled there, and made a living for himself by knitting and selling stockings.

Knitting was the source of many of Gotland's superstitions and folktales. It was believed that to knot the yarn inside a garment would bring bad luck to the wearer. Bad luck also would befall the person wearing a knitted garment with a pattern winding counterclockwise.

Legend tells of Bjorkume-Ole, who always wore a knitted skullcap on his head. The cap was very old and worn, and everyone thought Ole needed a new one. Ole, who was quite superstitious, believed he would live longer if his new cap were knitted by a young and innocent girl. Like

his old cap, the new one must be made of gray and black wool from the youngest sheep. It must have a pattern on the border, with the crown striped as the spokes of a wheel, and on top a tassle hanging down exactly to the ear. He finally received his new cap, but it never was worn. The rings of the wheel design had been knitted counter-clockwise. Ole believed he would never get to heaven if he wore that cap.

The importance of wool today

Today, knitting and commercial use of wool are not extensive on Gotland. Working with wool is no longer profitable, and sheep now are raised primarily for sheepskin garments. The rich tradition of working with wool, part of life on Gotland for many years, is disappearing; the old techniques and knowledge are nearly forgotten. When industry began to mass-produce knitted garments, it became unnecessary to hand knit stockings, mittens, caps and sweaters. The custom of passing down the old patterns from generation to generation ended and many are forever lost.

But recently there has been a revival of interest in preserving the old knowledge and traditions. Sheep owners are re-evaluating the commercial potential of wool. Better wool, suitable for yarn manufacturing, could be produced and wool production could again be a worthwhile occupation. Plans for a new woolen mill on Gotland are giving hope that the old knitting tradition on the island may continue and strengthen. The techniques and patterns which belong to Gotland have survived many generations. They portray the uniqueness of Gotland's natural history and reflect the island's way of life. It is important that people feel the connection between the traditions of yesteryear and today's technology.

Mittens and patterns from Gotland

Typical mittens from Gotland are knitted with a repeat pattern which continues even on the inside and outside of the thumb during the increasing and decreasing, and all the way to the fingertips. A different pattern, perhaps ivy, is often knitted at the wrist.

The traditional patterns have strong ties to nature on Gotland, and are referred to in an old folk song called "Out In Our Pasture":

> Come lilies and columbine,
> Come roses and sage,
> Come sweet mint,
> Come joy of the heart.

Ivy, rose bushes, rose wreaths, forget-me-nots, and lingon branches wind around the hand and thumb of the mitten. Frequently the old wheel pattern, in different formations, is used. Sometimes it's a sundial, sometimes there is a cross knitted between the wheels.

The colors, too, are copied from Gotland's natural environment. Brown and black for the background suggest stonemoss, walnut and oak bark. The bright colors in the patterns represent the island's beautiful wildflowers.

Traditionally, the date or the recipient's name or initials might be knitted into the cuff or body of the mitten. The cuff was sometimes knitted as a collar, which might extend all the way to the elbow. The collar was often knitted double thickness, with the same pattern on the inside as on the outside.

To achieve the firmness of a woven fabric, thin yarn and thin knitting needles were used. Felting of the knitted fabric also gave added firmness to the mittens and made them warmer and longer lasting.

Felting was most often done by washing the newly-knitted garment in soap and warm water, rubbing it against a washboard. Garments which were to be felted could be knitted more loosely, and a little larger, since they shrank during the felting process.

Knitting a pattern in two or more colors also made the mittens thicker and warmer. Using a multi-colored pattern offered the additional benefit of delighting the eye as the knitter watched the pattern emerge.

Sometimes, in an old pair of mittens, carefully mended holes can be seen. Mending was done with a small knitted patch, worked in a pattern which may or may not have been the same as that of the original mitten.

Use of the patterns on different garments

These traditional patterns were not used just for mittens. Stockings, caps, suspenders, sweaters, and different kinds of ribbon were adorned with the rose and ivy patterns that identified the garment's wearer as a Gotlander.

Sweaters were knitted in different ways. Everyday work sweaters were made of gray wool, thick and warm, often knitted in stockinette. Dressier sweaters might be of fine white wool, with roses or stripes, or any sort of figures knitted into them—columbine, hourglasses, vines, or hearts.

Carl von Linne, during his visit to Gotland in 1741, noted that "the farmers were generally wearing sweaters which were beautifully decorated with white, blue, and red colors, just as if they had been woven, though they actually were knitted by the hands of the farmers' wives." Another visitor to Gotland at that time wrote: "On Gotland, stockings, mittens and sweaters were knitted with flowers and in all kinds of colors—but without knots on the inside."

Special wedding stockings were knitted in white wool, with rose designs on the top part and a vine pattern above that. Sometimes the vine was ivy, Gotland's Provincial plant, which grows readily anywhere it gets a foothold, like a symbol for faithfulness. Wedding stockings were knitted with the softest wool, and had to be so pliable that, when rolled up, they could fit invisibly in the palm of the hand. Work stockings were knitted for thickness and warmth, and were often felted.

It was also quite the regular thing to knit suspenders, garters or just long ribbons to give a dear friend or fiance, or just to hang on the wall as decorations. The ribbons often had patterns of roses, vines, and animals, or of simple objects that were part of daily life.

Make Gotland's patterns today like they were done in the past, but according to your own taste and your own feelings. We chose to show all the patterns knitted on mittens, but they can be used on stockings, caps or sweaters just as well. You may want to use a border of roses on a sweater, for instance, or repeat a vine pattern all around the tops of a pair of stockings, or let a row of birds fly around the border of a cap.

To knit mittens

Two balls of wool and a set of 5 double-pointed knitting needles are all you need to knit a pair of mittens.

The yarn we have used is a single-ply (baby-weight) wool, such as Berga upholstery yarn or Marks Faro; and two-ply (fingering) wool such as Berga Knitting Yarn Extra, Blanket yarn, Pakoyarn, or mohair. Knitting needles #0 or smaller are suitable for the single-ply yarn and #0 or #1 for the two-ply yarn. If you use a set of 4 double-pointed needles, you'll need to revise these instructions accordingly.

If you want to knit a pair of especially nice, pliable mittens, choose a thin yarn. The pattern will then be very pretty since so many pattern repeats will fit within the high stitch count which will result.

When a plain stockinette stitch cuff is desired, it is advisable to work the first few rows in a rib stitch to avoid having the edge roll up.

The number of stitches in the cuff and hand of the mitten—including the thumb—must be a multiple of the number of stitches in the pattern repeat.

If the pattern requires that one of the yarns must be carried over more than 5 stitches, twist the yarns around each other (in a half-hitch) to avoid having long, loose strands on the back side.

When you need to increase or decrease, do it between the cuff and body of the mitten and when the pattern changes, so it won't be as noticeable.

Adult's mitten

Instructions are for single-ply wool, with the number of stitches for two-ply wool in parentheses.

Materials needed for a pair of mittens knitted with:
  Single-ply wool - about 50 grams (25 grams of each color)
  Two-ply wool - about 100 grams (50 grams of each color)

- Select the cuff and hand patterns you want to knit.
- Note the number of stitches in one pattern repeat for the style you've chosen. Let this determine the number of stitches needed for the mitten keeping in mind the actual hand measurement. The hand of an adult's mitten, excluding the cuff, should usually measure about 7¼ to 8" long and about 4" wide.
- Determine the number of stitches needed for the cuff and cast on. An adult's mitten requires about 84-100 (56-64) stitches for the cuff and 96-112 (72-84) stitches for the hand. Knit the cuff to the desired length.
- After the cuff is complete, knit the body of the mitten, in the pattern you've chosen, to the point where the thumb begins— about 2½ to 3¼".
- For the thumb, place about the first 18-22 (14-16) stitches from the first needle onto a stitch holder or safety pin. On the next round, again cast on the same number of stitches as are on the holder. Remember that the number of stitches for the thumb also must be a multiple of the number of stitches in your pattern repeat.
- Continue knitting until you reach almost to the top of the little finger. Then begin decreasing. Start by decreasing at every other row or every third row. At about the top of the index finger, begin to decrease every row. To decrease, at the beginning of the first needle (slip 1, knit 1, pass slipped stitch over), then knit the last 2 stitches on the second needle together. Repeat on the third and fourth needles. When approximately 10 stitches are left, cut the yarn and pull it through the remaining stitches. Pull firmly and secure the end.
- Transfer the stitches for the thumb from the stitch holder onto 2 needles. Pick up the same number of stitches as are on the cast-on edge above the thumb and place on 2 needles. Continuing with the 5 needles, knit the thumb to the point where the nail begins. Then work decreases to the top of the thumb, in the same manner as for the hand, until approximately 6 stitches are left.

Child's mitten in single-ply wool

Instructions are given for size 1-2 (3-4/5-7) years.

- Select the cuff and hand patterns you want to knit.
- Note the number of stitches in one pattern repeat for the style you've chosen. Let this determine the number of stitches needed for the mitten keeping in mind the actual hand measurement. A child's hand measures about 3¾" (4¼/5") and the width for the mitten should be about 2½" (3/3½").
- Determine the number of stitches needed for the cuff and cast on. A child's mitten knit with single-ply yarn requires about 56 (60/68) stitches for the cuff and 64 (72/76) stitches for the hand. Knit the cuff to the desired length.
- After the cuff is complete, knit the body of the mitten, in the pattern you've chosen, to the point where the thumb begins— about 1¼ (1¼/1½").
- For the thumb, place about the first 12 (14/16) stitches from the first needle onto a stitch holder or safety pin. On the next round, again cast on the same number of stitches as are on the holder. Remember that the number of stitches for the thumb also must be a multiple of the number of stitches in your pattern repeat.
- Continue knitting until you reach almost to the top of the little finger—about 1½" (2/2½"). Then begin decreasing. Start by decreasing at every other row or every third row. At about the top of the index finger, begin to decrease every row. To decrease, at the beginning of the first needle (slip 1, knit 1, pass slipped stitch over), then knit the last 2 stitches on the second needle together. Repeat on the third and fourth needles. When approximately 8 stitches are left, cut the yarn and pull it through the remaining stitches. Pull firmly and secure the end.
- Transfer the stitches for the thumb from the stitch holder onto 2 needles. Pick up the same number of stitches as are on the cast-on edge above the thumb and place on 2 needles. Continuing with the 5 needles, knit the thumb to the point where the nail begins—about 1" (1¼/1½"). Then work decreases to the top of the thumb, in the same manner as for the hand, until approximately 6 stitches are left.

Child's mitten in two-ply wool

Instructions are given for size 1-2 (3-4/5-7) years.

- Select the cuff and hand patterns you want to knit.
- Note the number of stitches in one pattern repeat for the style you've chosen. Let this determine the number of stitches needed for the mitten keeping in mind the actual hand measurement. A child's hand measures about 3¾" (4¼/5") and the width for the mitten should be about 2½" (3/3½").
- Determine the number of stitches needed for the cuff and cast on. A child's mitten knit with two-ply yarn requires about 40 (44/48) stitches for the cuff and 48 (48/52) for the hand. Knit the cuff to the desired length.
- After the cuff is complete, knit the body of the mitten, in the pattern you've chosen, to the point where the thumb begins— about 1¼" (1¼/1½").
- For the thumb, place about the first 9 (11/12) stitches from the first needle onto a stitch holder or safety pin. On the next round, again cast on the same number of stitches as are on the holder. Remember that the number of stitches for the thumb also must be a multiple of the number of stitches in your pattern repeat.
- Continue knitting until you reach almost to the top of the little finger—about 1½" (2/2½"). Then begin decreasing. Start by decreasing at every other row or every third row. At about the top of the index finger, begin to decrease every row. To decrease, at the beginning of the first needle (slip 1, knit 1, pass slipped stitch over), then knit the last 2 stitches on the second needle together. Repeat on the third and fourth needles. When approximately 8 stitches are left, cut the yarn and pull it through the remaining stitches. Pull firmly and secure the end.
- Transfer the stitches for the thumb from the stitch holder onto 2 needles. Pick up the same number of stitches as are on the cast-on edge above the thumb and place on 2 needles. Continuing with the 5 needles, knit the thumb to the point where the nail begins—about 1" (1¼/1½"). Then work decreases to the top of the thumb, in the same manner as for the hand, until approximately 6 stitches are left.

Rose pattern

From Burs

Pattern repeat 12 stitches

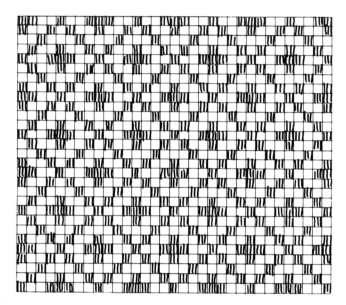

Old goose-eye pattern

Pattern repeat 8 stitches

Forget-me-not

From Tofta

Pattern repeat 10 stitches

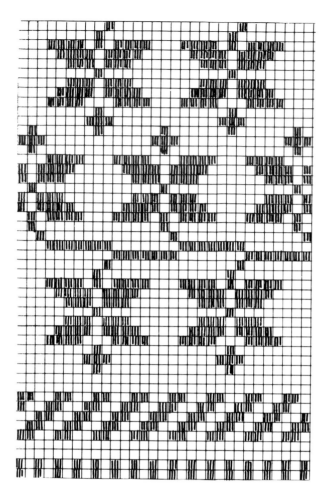

Leaf pattern

From about 1850

Stripes at the bottom first are 2-stitch repeat, then 4-stitch repeat

Leaf pattern repeat 14 stitches

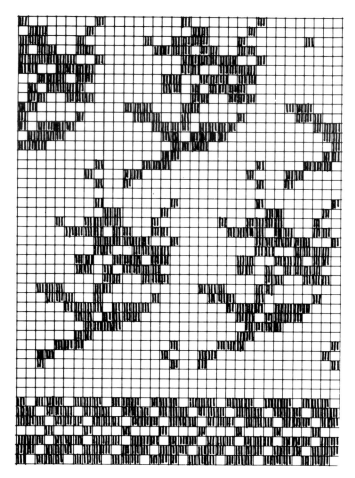

Flower branches

Vine pattern on cuff, 4-stitch repeat

Flower branch pattern, 17-stitch repeat

Sundial

From southern Gotland

Pattern repeat 22 stitches

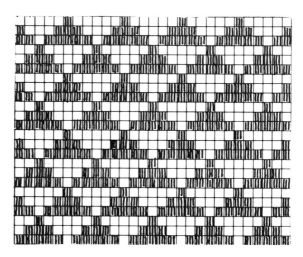

Night and day

Pattern repeat 6 stitches

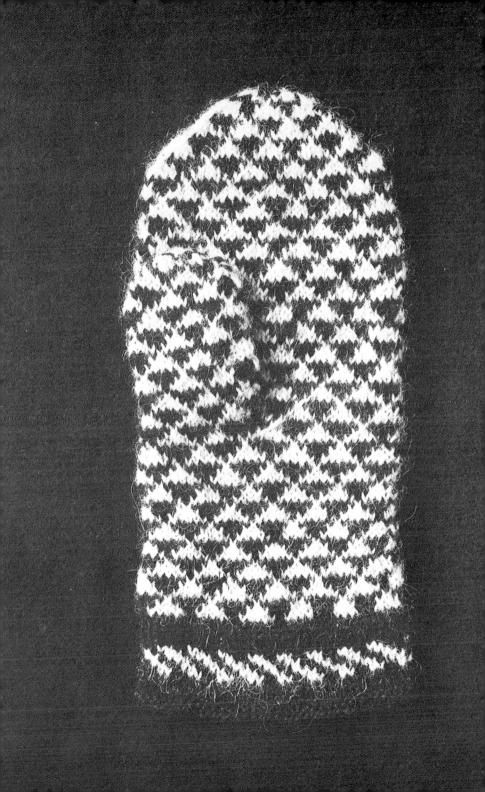

Branch and squares

Pattern repeat 32 stitches

Rosepole

Pattern from Tofta

Pattern repeat 12 stitches

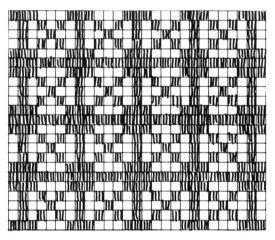

Pattern from Gammelgarn

Pattern repeat 6 stitches

Four-leaf clover

Pattern repeat 14 stitches

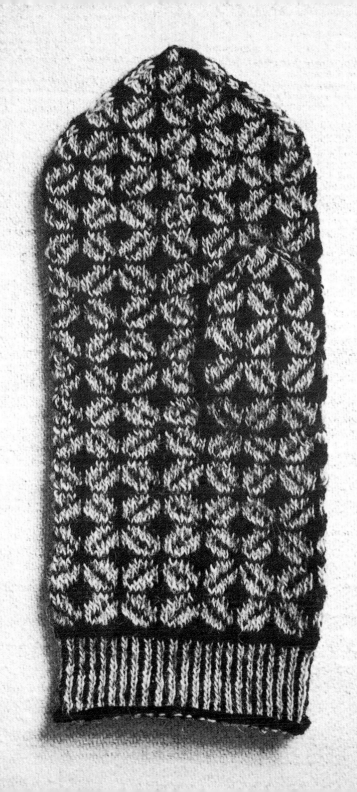

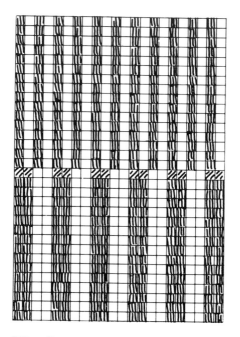

Pole pattern

Pattern repeat for wide stripe is 4 stitches (last row is purled), for narrow stripe is 2 stitches

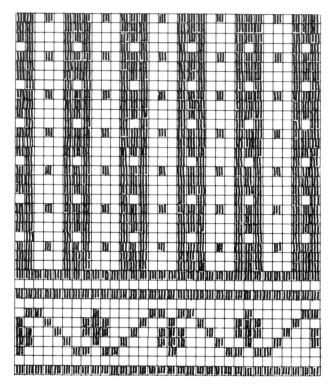

Pole pattern

From Gammelgarn

Cuff pattern is copied from suspenders dated 1835.

Cuff pattern repeat 16 stitches

Pole pattern repeat 6 stitches

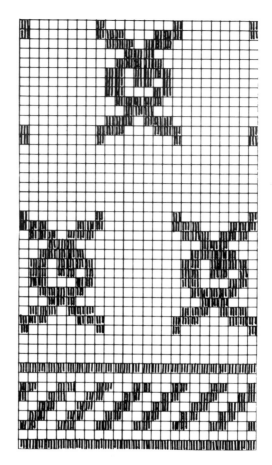

Rose pattern

From a knitted garter, dated about 1860

Cuff pattern repeat 4 stitches

Rose pattern repeat 16 stitches

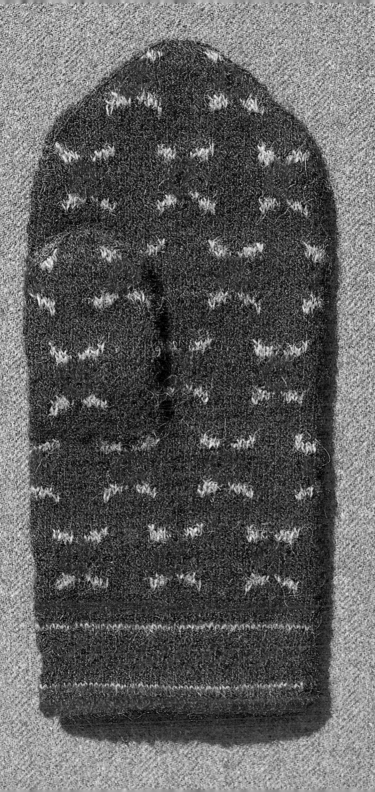

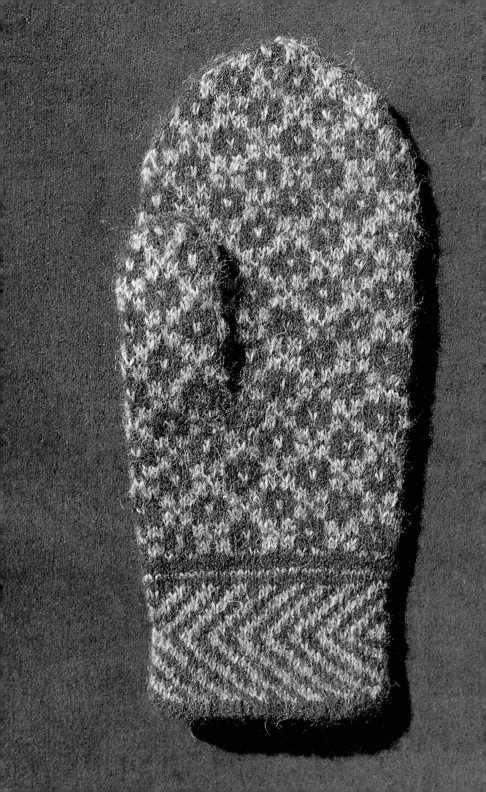

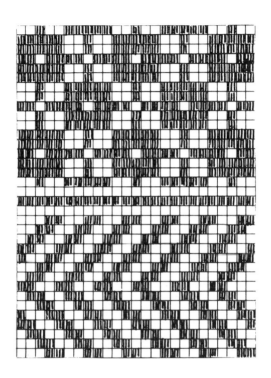

Rose wreath

Cuff pattern repeat 4 stitches

Wreath pattern repeat 10 stitches

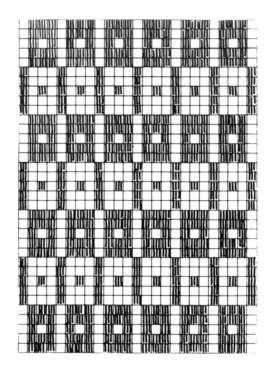

Broken pole pattern

Pattern repeat 4 stitches

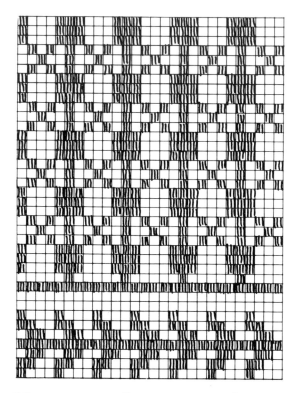

Pattern from Tofta

Vine pattern repeat above cuff is 4 stitches

Main pattern repeat is 6 stitches

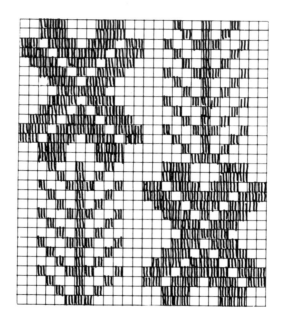

Pattern from Guldrupe

Pattern at bottom of mitten first is 2-stitch repeat, then 4-stitch repeat

Main pattern repeat 13 stitches

Checkered pattern

From Bro

Vine pattern repeat 6 stitches

Border above vine pattern, 4-stitch repeat

Checkered pattern repeat 10 stitches

Rose pattern

Pattern repeat 6 stitches

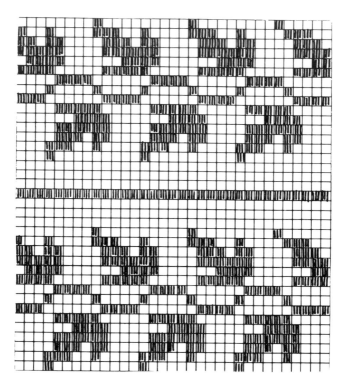

Ivy pattern

From knitted suspenders
Pattern repeat 10 stitches

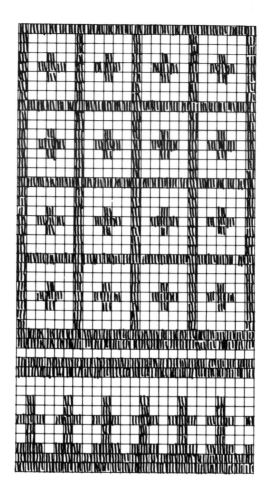

Clover

From Bro

Cuff pattern is called "upside-down lily"

Cuff pattern repeat 4 stitches

Clover pattern repeat 6 stitches

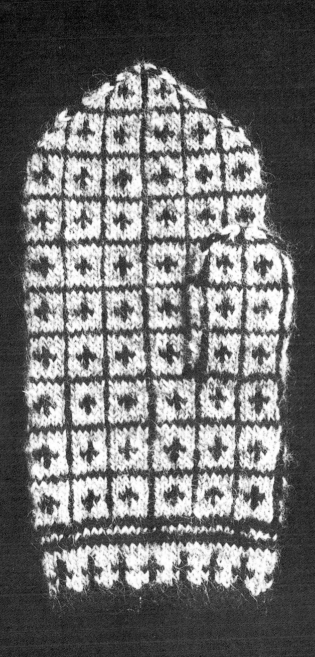

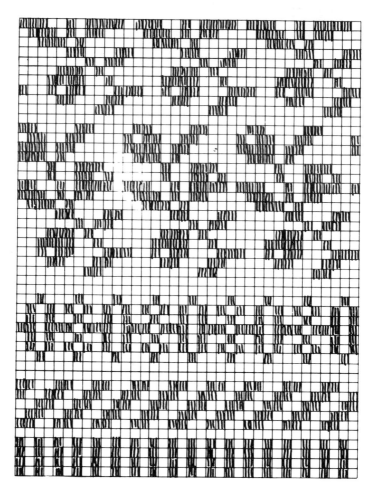

Lingonberry

From church mittens from Alskig, 1885

Stripes at bottom first are 2-stitch repeat, then
4-stitch repeat

Cuff pattern repeat 8 stitches

Lingonberry pattern repeat 12 stitches

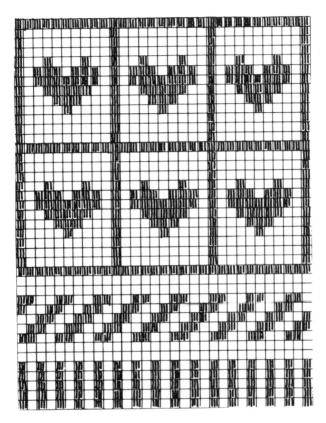

Heart

From Bro

Stripes on cuff first are 2-stitch repeat, then 4-stitch repeat

Heart pattern repeat 10 stitches

Pattern from Hangvar

Pattern repeat 4 stitches

Checkered pattern

From Halla

Pattern repeat 10 stitches

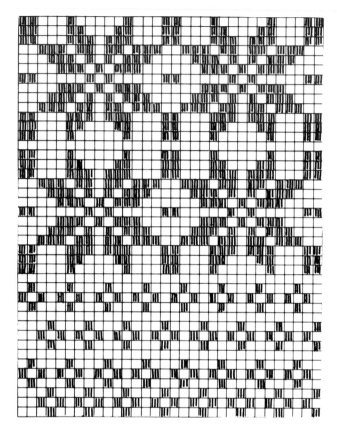

Stars

Pattern repeat on cuff 4 stitches

Star pattern repeat 15 stitches

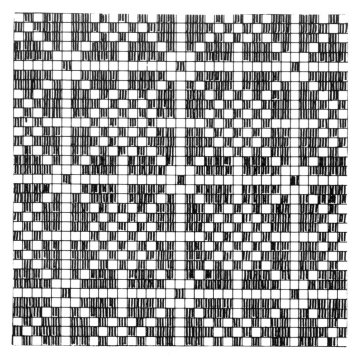

Sundial

Pattern repeat 12 stitches

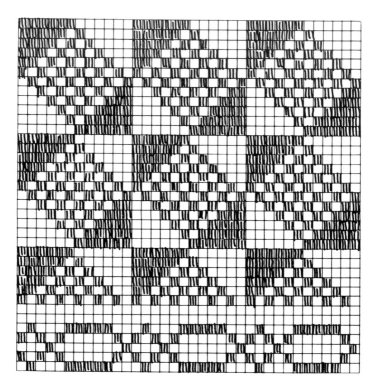

Hourglass

Pattern repeat 12 stitches

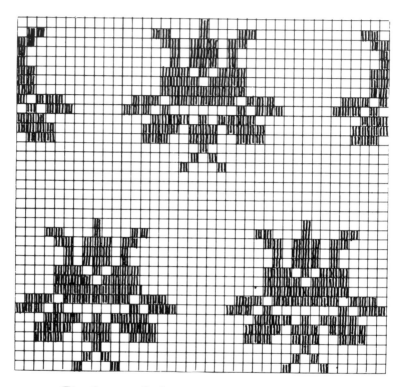

Columbine

Pattern from the 1700s

Pattern repeat 22 stitches

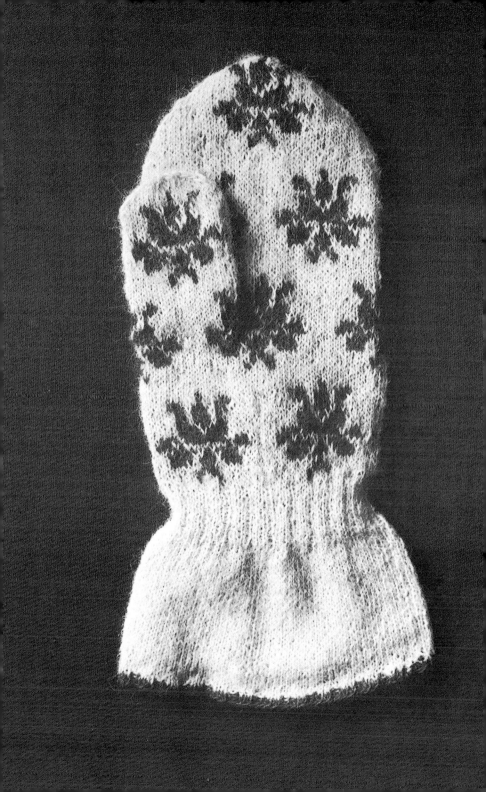

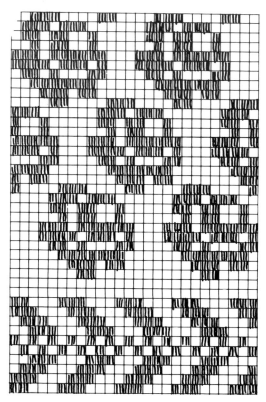

Roses

Pattern from about 1850

Vine pattern on cuff is 6-stitch repeat

Rose pattern repeat 13 stitches

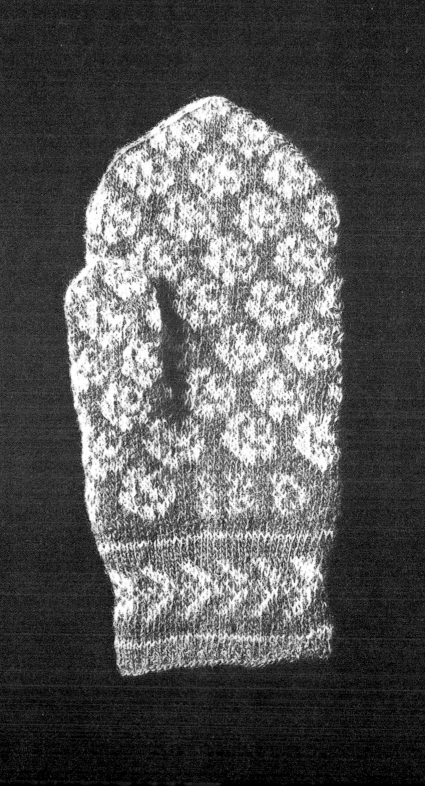

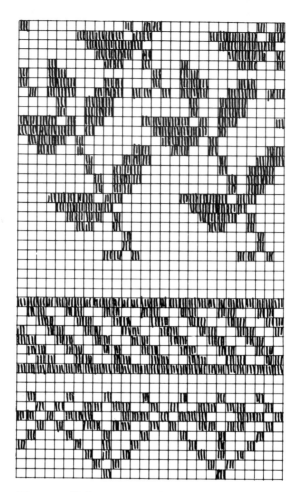

Leaf branches

Cuff pattern repeat 12 stitches

Border above cuff, 4-stitch repeat

Branch pattern repeat 14 stitches

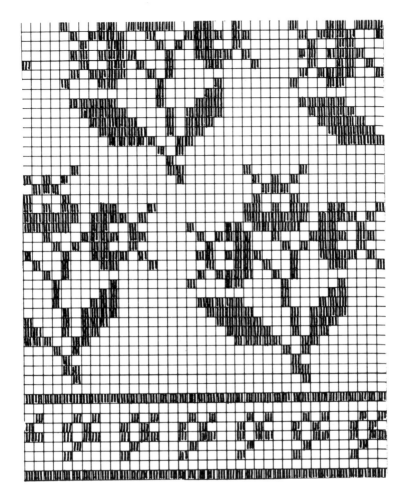

Flowers

Pattern copied from wedding stockings knitted in Stanga in 1860

Cuff pattern repeat 6 stitches

Flower pattern repeat 24 stitches

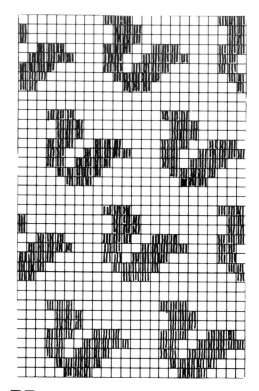

Horseshoe

From about 1850

Pattern repeat 12 stitches

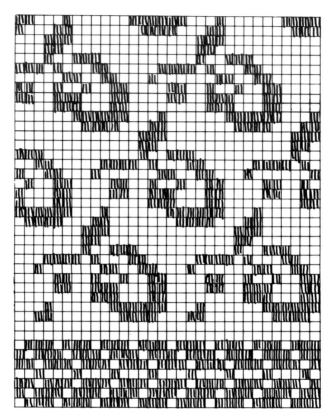

Pattern from a stocking border

Vine pattern repeat 4 stitches

Main pattern repeat 16 stitches

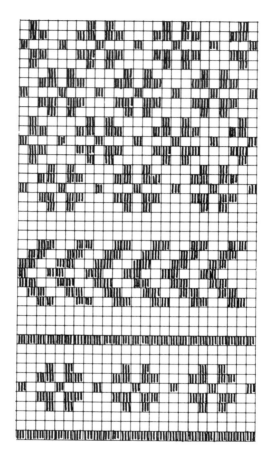

Small star pattern

Cuff pattern repeat 8 stitches

Border above cuff pattern, 4-stitch repeat

Star pattern repeat 8 stitches

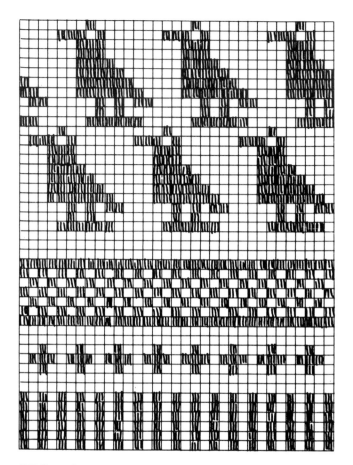

Birds

Stripes on cuff are 2-stitch repeat

Pattern above stripes, 4-stitch repeat

Checkered cuff pattern repeat 2 stitches

Bird pattern repeat 11 stitches

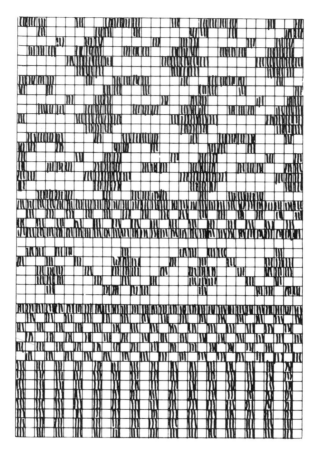

Waves

Checkered and striped patterns on cuff both are
2-stitch repeats

Wave pattern repeat 10 stitches

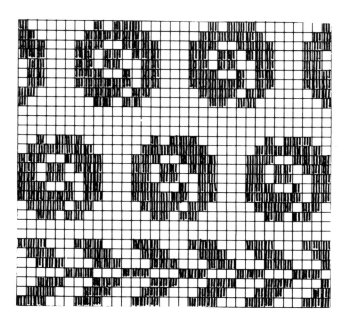

Roses from Rone

Vine pattern repeat 6 stitches

Rose pattern repeat 12 stitches

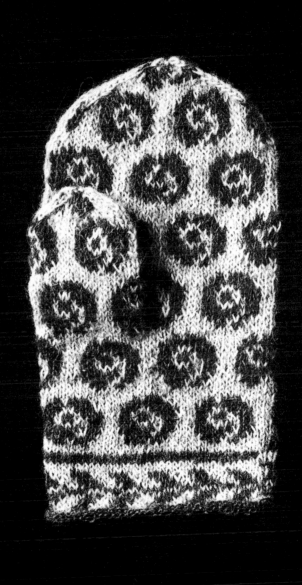

Snowstar

Checkered pattern repeat 2 stitches

Cuff pattern repeat 4 stitches

Snowstar pattern repeat 12 stitches